CORE WRITING SKILLS

How to
Write a Narrative

Sara Howell

PowerKids
press™

New York

Published in 2014 by The Rosen Publishing Group, Inc.
29 East 21st Street, New York, NY 10010

First Edition

Editor: Amelie von Zumbusch
Book Design: Andrew Povolny
Photo Research: Katie Stryker

Photo Credits: Cover Stockbyte/Getty Images; p. 4 Odua Images/Shutterstock.com; p. 5 Fotokostic/ Shutterstock.com; pp. 6–7, 18–19, 22 Monkey Business Images/Shutterstock.com; p. 8 BestPhotoStudio/ Shutterstock.com; p. 9 Julie Keen/Shutterstock.com; p. 10 PLRANG/Shutterstock.com; pp. 12–13 Todd S. Holder/Shutterstock.com; p. 14 Andy Dean Photography/Shutterstock.com; p. 16 Digital Media Pro/ Shutterstock.com; p. 20 Dejan Ristovski/Shutterstock.com; p. 21 Rob Marmion/Shutterstock.com.

Library of Congress Cataloging-in-Publication Data

Howell, Sara.
  How to write a narrative / by Sara Howell. — First edition.
    pages cm. — (Core Writing Skills)
  Includes index.
  ISBN 978-1-4777-2908-3 (library) — ISBN 978-1-4777-2997-7 (pbk.) —
ISBN 978-1-4777-3067-6 (6-pack)
  1. Authorship—Juvenile literature. 2. Creative writing—Juvenile literature. I. Title.
PN159.H69 2014
  808.02—dc23
                                2013022407

Manufactured in the United States of America

CPSIA Compliance Information: Batch #W14PK4: For Further Information contact Rosen Publishing, New York, New York at 1-800-237-9932

CONTENTS

WHAT IS A NARRATIVE?

A narrative is a piece of writing that tells a story. Narratives are written for people to enjoy while reading them. They can also teach lessons, or morals. Some narratives, called **fiction**, are about imagined, or made-up, people and events. Other narratives tell true stories that really happened to the writer. These are called personal narratives.

A personal narrative often describes an interesting adventure that a writer had. For example, it can be fun to read about a writer's exciting trip!

Stories that include imaginary creatures, such as dragons, are fiction.

Writing Tip

Fictional stories are often written in a style called third person, in which characters are often referred to as "he," "she," and "they."

Narrative writing gives you the freedom to make many choices. Your narrative can be as long or as short as you like. The story can take place over just a few minutes or over many years. When you write a narrative, you are in charge!

WHO'S WHO

All narratives are about individuals, called **characters**. Your characters can be people, animals, space aliens, or anything else you can imagine! Your story can have just one character or many. A character who explains to the reader what is happening is called the **narrator**.

Introduce your main characters at the beginning of the story. Use **details** to show readers why a character is different or special. You could write that Mr. Jenkins is the town librarian or that Greta is the tallest girl in her school. Spend some time thinking about who your characters are before you begin writing.

Writing Tip

In a short narrative, it is a good idea to have just a few characters. Too many characters can confuse readers.

Explain how the characters in your story know each other. Are they friends, siblings, neighbors, or something else entirely?

CREATING CONFLICT

Once you have characters, your story will need a **conflict**, or problem. For example, your character Michael could find out that his best friend is moving or that his mother is having another baby. Your character's actions will create the **plot**, or events of the story. After each event, ask yourself, what would Michael do next?

Sometimes, a character in a narrative needs to make an important decision. This can provide the conflict that drives the story's plot.

The plot should unfold in a clear and natural event **sequence**. A sequence is the order in which things happen. The better you know your character's thoughts and feelings, the easier it will be to decide what he would do after each new event.

Some people like plots with a lot of exciting action, while others like low-key plots about everyday life. Which do you prefer?

DESCRIPTIVE DETAILS

Strong narrative writing uses many effective **techniques**, or ways of doing things. One of these techniques is using **descriptive** details to help readers picture a person or a place. If you were to say, "Ms. Withers was ugly," different readers might imagine the character in many different ways. Instead you could write, "Ms. Withers had

Remember to include descriptive details about the places in which your story is set, too.

The best birthday present was a surprise visit from my dad. I was eating the (chocolate-chip pancakes) that my grandfather had made (when I heard) (three loud knocks) on the door. I opened the door and my dad stood there on our (newly painted porch.)

yellow, rotting teeth and a giant red blister on her forehead." These descriptive details give readers a clear image of the character.

Descriptive details can also include more than just what you see. Use all five of your senses to describe the world of your story!

Writing Tip

To describe something, you can compare it to something else. For example, you could write, "Ms. Withers's breath smelled like a wet dog."

SHOWING ACTION

To keep your story moving forward, it needs to have action. Words that show action, such as "run" and "jump," are called **verbs**. Good action words give readers a clear picture of what a character does and how he feels.

It is often more interesting to show actions instead of explaining feelings. The sentence "Marcus was bored" tells readers how a character feels as he sits in class. Instead you could write, "Marcus watched the ticking clock. He tapped his pencil on his desk." Readers will be able to guess from Marcus's actions that he was bored.

Writing Tip

Most fiction and personal narratives are written in the past tense, as though they have already happened.

What verbs would you use to describe the actions of the boy in this picture?

SPEAK UP!

People often share their thoughts and feelings by talking. The characters in your story should get the chance to speak, too! When characters talk to each other, it is called **dialogue**. Like action words, dialogue lets you show, instead of tell, what a character is thinking or feeling.

Dialogue is a great way to show readers your characters' opinions. After all, you can learn a lot about what a person feels or thinks by talking to him.

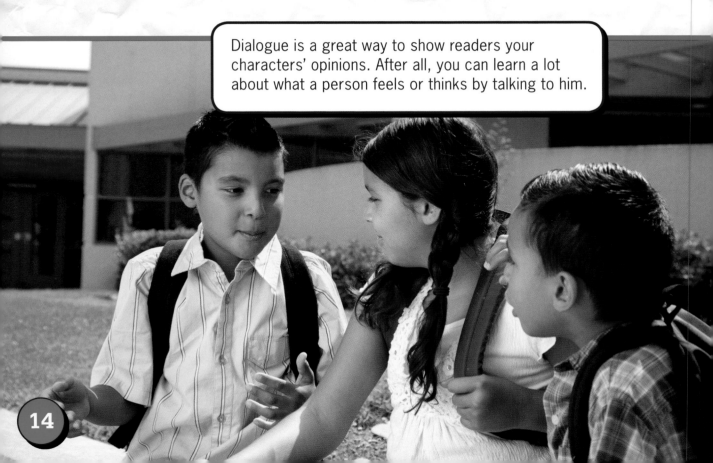

"See you at the top!" Sam called down from the ladder.

Alex winced. "I am actually afraid of heights," he admitted.

"Why didn't you say so?" Sam said. "Let's go swimming instead."

Dialogue tags

Quotation marks

Writing dialogue that sounds real takes practice. The next time you are on the bus or waiting in line, listen to the people around you. Pay attention to how they speak and the words they use. Try writing down interesting things you hear and putting those lines of dialogue in your story!

Writing Tip

Lines of dialogue are put in double quotation marks. Each time a new character speaks, start a new paragraph.

TEMPORAL WORDS

As events occur in your story, it is important to show the order in which they happen clearly. **Temporal words** can help you do that. The word "temporal" means "having to do with time." Temporal words are words that show time, such as "first," "next," and "after." Temporal words give readers signals, or hints, about the story's event sequence.

Temporal words are useful when describing what happened at a sports event, such as a soccer game.

After making sure that the coast was clear, Lily and Max tiptoed toward the boat. Lily climbed in first. Max followed. Then they paddled away before anyone could notice that they had escaped!

Temporal words are useful as **transitions** between paragraphs. Try starting a new paragraph with a temporal phrase such as "the next day" or "after that." This shows readers that time has passed between the last event and the next one.

Writing Tip

Before you begin writing, draw a diagram of your story's events. Fill in boxes with things that happen "first," "next," "then," and "last."

ENDING YOUR STORY

The way a story ends is just as important as how it begins. Try to give readers a sense of closure, or a satisfied feeling. Did your character get what she wanted? Did she learn any lessons?

One effective technique is to end your story with a strong feeling, image, or action.

Writing Tip

Some writers know how their stories will end before they begin writing. Others discover their endings as they write. See what works for you!

Say your story is about Alex's best friend moving away. Your narrative could end with the sentence "Alex smiled and looked at the letter in his hand one more time before he dropped it in the mailbox." Readers feel closure knowing that Alex is happy and will keep in touch with his friend.

Do you like stories that end happily? Such narratives sometimes end with the words "and they lived happily ever after."

USING TECHNOLOGY

Technology, such as computers and tablets, makes writing and sharing your narratives easier than ever before. Computers allow you to go back and edit, or change, parts of your story without rewriting the whole thing by hand. Certain computer programs will also point out spelling and grammar mistakes.

When your story is finished, use email to send it to friends

It can be fun to write a narrative with your friends. Using a computer makes it easy to work together.

and family members who live far away. With your parents' permission, look online for writing contests you can enter. Do not just worry about winning, though. Remember, stories are written so they can be read and enjoyed by others!

If you want to share a story with family members who live far away, just email it to them!

21

Narrative writing can be a lot of fun. When you write a story, you decide who and what it will be about. You can write about your own life or create new worlds!

Reading narratives by other people can help you become a better writer. Think about the characters, event sequence, and descriptive details in your favorite book. Did the author use a certain technique that you liked? When you write your own stories, use what you have learned from others' strengths and mistakes!

Some people like reading personal narratives, while others like reading stories about the future. What kinds of narratives do you like?

GLOSSARY

characters (KER-ik-turz) People in a story.

conflict (KON-flikt) A fight or struggle.

descriptive (dih-SKRIP-tiv) Using words to give a picture.

details (dih-TAYLZ) Extra facts.

dialogue (DY-uh-lawg) Part of a written work with two or more characters speaking.

fiction (FIK-shun) Stories that tell about people and events that are not real.

narrator (NA-ray-tur) A character who tells a story.

plot (PLOT) The events that happen in a story.

sequence (SEE-kwens) The order in which actions take place.

techniques (tek-NEEKS) Ways of doing things.

temporal words (TEM-puh-rul WURDZ) Words that have to do with time.

transitions (tran-SIH-shunz) Ways of changing or passing from one thing to another.

verbs (VERBZ) Word that describe actions.

INDEX

WEBSITES

Due to the changing nature of Internet links, PowerKids Press has developed an online list of websites related to the subject of this book. This site is updated regularly. Please use this link to access the list: www.powerkidslinks.com/cws/narr/